Religious

Really Jesus

By

Deluke Muwanigwa

COPYRIGHT @ 2021   RELIGIOUS (Really Jesus)
by Deluke Muwanigwa

Published by Poetry Planet Book Publishing House
Arranged by Tess Ritumalta
Edited by Marie Ezekiel

ISBN;
Softbound/Paperback-978-621-8261-94-5
Hardbound-978-621-8261-95-2
Mobile/Kindle-978-621-8261-96-9

Photos used were taken from Pinterest and may contain their own copyrights

ACKNOWLEDGEMENT

I would like to thank the publisher of Poetry Planet Publishing House for agreeing to publish these poems. Publish a divergent view to your own is the height of professionalism. I would also like to acknowledge my poetry peers who have reviewed my poems and made guarded comments seeing they enjoyed the poesy but not necessarily the message. My friend Robert Murray Smith of Australia in particular.

PREFACE

Religion is an emotive subject. Proponents of religion protect their faith with their lives, notwithstanding that there are 405 religions, each claiming to be. Taboo subjects are a poet's playground and religion is one of those subjects poets will devote time to, either because they subscribe to the tenets or they are critical of certain aspects of the teachings. This book is about the poet's own understanding or lack therefore of religion and I hope the reader will read with an open mind.

TABLE OF CONTENTS

ABSURDITIES

It's absurd that a race exists because one person
laughed at his father
It's absurd that five thousand people were fed with one
loaf of bread
Its absurd wine was made from water without yeast
It's absurd that someone who died was resurrected
Surely he must have been in a coma.
It cannot be repeated because it's impossible.
And yet millions of people base their lives on fiction
No wonder we have so much friction.
No wonder there is racism
No wonder there is fascism
Faith-based delusions are a danger to humanity
Claiming to work for commonality.
Oddities
Absurdities.

A BLACK DAY

Today was one of those black days
Got home in pitch blackness
Welcomed by a power blackout
The food I forgot on the stove had burnt black
I groped in the dark so black
Could not find the knob to my black door
And dropped my Blackberry black phone in the black
night.
My bed I missed bed sheets being black
In the darkness so black
Having taken some Carling Black Label
And Johnnie Walker Red Label mixed with Black
I collapsed on my black leather sofa
And blacked out
A black day

ACT

Act

Alaskan Alastair lacked fact and tact
Alas, his attack was due to a lack of tract in his abstract
He was accused of plagiarism
The word being antidisestablishmentarianism.

Act

A fact remains even after the act
Is attacked due to lack of tact
Stick to your gun
Even for fun
You never know who you may attract

A-bove all when you read the Bible
C-helsea FC distracting you by ball
T-urn to facts in pages of 'ACTS'

BIG BANG

In the beginning, there was a big bang

This is contrary to what the Bible says

Our young star sun exploded into pieces

Our nine planets flung out to form our solar system

This is reality happening now not a thesis

Different planets some rocky some you see steam

Our earth a safe distance from our thermonuclear bomb

Which our sun is; can support life

Other planets too near or too far from the fission
hydrogen bomb,

Which is our sun, cannot support life

There are trillions of stars out there in the universe

Some so young born seconds ago some ready to
explode

God is making and continues to create worlds even
multiverse

If we keep polluting our only world called earth it will
implode

We will destroy our life-giving earth made by God

Due to our greed, consumption, and love for Gold.

BIG BANG BAND

He banged the big bang like a band
To make the earth, broke a star mixed with sand
We thank our Father
Made Eve and brother
Now we just bang, destroying our own land

BIG BURLY BULLY

The big burly bully bullied the poor boy
Forced him to give up his favourite toy
Boy tried not to cry
To be manly he tried
An uppercut cut the bully's trip to Troy

DEAD

He searched for days on end,
Deep in his heart's chambers,
For an iota of forgiveness.
There was none.
His aorta spewed renewed anger. Enraged every time
he thought of the incident.
That incident.

At their usual rendezvous,
At the edge of the park they met.
Young impish boys hardly teenaged. Bundles of
perpetual motion.
Always causing a commotion.

His sibling brother was there. Savouring the impossible
happening, possibly the architect of covert instigation.
The big burly bully walked up close, pulled his clothes,
And declared, "I hate you!"

Before he could comprehend from whence the enmity
had derived in his equanimity,
Stars were going round his head. Imaginary birds
tweeting in his ears. Another hard meteoric impact to
his eye and he fell into a deep ditch. Dazed.

A grounds man, watching the scene in disbelief,
Came charging to break up the fight. Nay, the drubbing
to be honestly honest.

So, there was no reason to forgive.
To forgive the sibling brother for setting him up to
satisfy sadistic pleasures.

No remorse.

So, no wonder he could not forgive. So, he loathed his
sibling brother.
So, loathed him for life.

So, he drove him a knife
Life on ice
Not really nice
Dead.

BIG BURLY BULLY PULLED

Big burly bully was hoisted up on a pulley
To a great height, clear night stars shining fully
He was full of fright
When rope pulled tight
Hangman ignored the bully, walked away coolly

THE GOOD BUSINESS OF GOD

The good business of God gets sown with weeds
Everyone thinking of Him according to needs
Yet we are all blessed
Though we act all messed

Each has been given a chance to enjoy free air
To carry a beautiful piece of God's hair
God's face, His spirit, and His image
In our competition to live differences emerge

We sow hatred, discrimination, and prejudice
Drifting from Him and His privileges
The good business of God gets sown with weeds
We pay dearly for drifting from His creed.

Let's all change our wayward ways
And love each as our God says

CONCEITED

The enemy of your enemy is your friend
This is quoted as a universal trend
Why is there so much enmity on earth?
One race wishing another race death
One tribe wishing another annihilation
One brother wishing another assimilation

Naming enemies has become an art
Let's name them up from the start
We have enemies just being enemies
Then the ubiquitous frenemies
Of the love-hate hate love dichotomy
Being the main feature of their anatomy

Permenemies are the next level
There is no scope for another label
A permenemy is hated and full stop
Wherever you meet its hate even at shops
A girlenemy hates all girls long they are not males
The person believes they cause gales
Then the boyonemies are the opposite
Believe boys are toads and composite
The queer is the LGBTonemy truly
Believe anyone different is foolish

Human beings a conceited lot
Quick to unfairly judge to win a plot
They have created fake pseudonyms
Even created opposite antonyms

The enemy of your enemy is my friend
Because I have no enemy I am afraid

Takes way much less energy to love
Than hate and be conceited like some.

CONFESSION

Confession

Been to the shebeen with Queen of Sheba
Imbibed with Bible in Beersheba
Did my confession
In a place of sin
Left, told Q of S will never see her

Confession

Completely false above poem
Over my dead body do I pour 'em
Not at the shebeen any way
First, I want to say now today
First, I want to kneel and pray
Even as I sin today every day
Satan is there but he is a liar
Satan is there using the crier
In every place even in church
Over there where God I search
Now for the confession "I did"

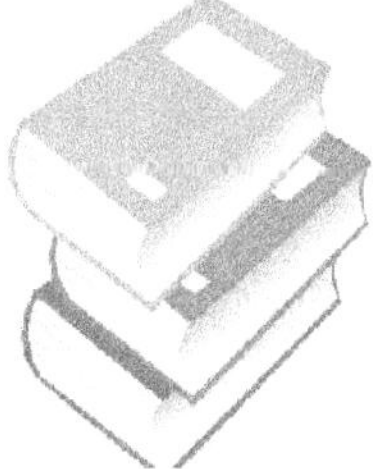

CONFESSIONALS

Confessionals

A man dreaded confessionals
Went to church eating confectionery
He had toffees
Hidden in office
In his bible a sweets dictionary

Confessionals

Conrad, confused, went for confessionals
Seeing he was tense, the pastor gave him confectionery
When his time came to confess
He admitted it was true his name was Conrad

Confessionals

Complete honesty
On confessionals
Not absolutely necessary
For even the preacher man
Even as he forgives you
Sins just as badly if not more
Sins he pretends he does not do
In the meantime he wants purity
Over and above your foibles
Normal white lies are regarded
As not sins per se
Let them go leniently
Silly confessionals!

CROSS

When I am cross I do the crossword puzzle.
I come across as a benign ass wearing a muzzle
My mind crisscrosses to the realm of life and death
The Cross, the Crucifix
Across, my tormentor sits arms crossed, gleefully
grinning.

Mr. Cross keeps harping on about the future looking
bright.
He makes me really cross with his selfishness. While he
lives large I eat promises and cross buns. A mercenary
with crossbones emblazoned on his soul.

One day I shall become so cross of Mr. Cross I shall pull
hard on the crossbow and escape across the oceans.
Cross my heart.

DARK URGES

In the dark is where it's at
Seeing no evil being primeval
Basically basing deeds on instinct
Black skin melding with the ambiance
Eyes at the tip of the fingers groping
In that beautiful state of artificial emptiness
Reminiscent of the dark ages
Are the dark urges
Faith and fate

Fate beyond faith
Faith beyond fate
The dichotomy

There is no doubt we are here
On this earth
Till death

We need good food
We need clean air
We need water

Items in short supply
We need to conserve
To use smart technology

But we spend our time destroying
Using harmful chemicals
Destroying ourselves

On Sundays, we bundle our kids
Dressed well to go to pray

Minding our faith

There is fate beyond faith
To live well while you live
To others love to give

We prefer faith beyond fate
Destroying our world
As if there is another

FAITH IS DANGEROUS

I am not being cantankerous
Before you shout "Heathen"
Read me out even

Hitler went to war based on faith
For his race of Aryans with a particular face
We know how that ended
German Law has been amended

Faith musk

Colonists went round the world pillaging
Be knighting with Bible the heathen in villages
Murder, rape, torture, and war
Contradicting their faith even more

Nine-eleven was caused by religious extremism
The West believes in capitalism expansionism
The perpetrators believing invaders were infidels
The West had faith they could subdue the impudent.

I am afraid of faith
An irrational belief in some fact
Draped in an aura and a face mask
A faith musk

GOD HELP US!

Out of dire need, I went to the high offices of those we
stood in winding queues to elect.
You know, the representatives of the people, by the
people, for the people, of our democracy
I found a democracy

An alien outlier society of people so detached from our
lives.
People with heads above the clouds
Too proud to stoop down low
And talk to me sitting on a cobbled floor
The chair and settee embossed in gold too precious for
me to sit.

The list
Conspicuous consumption
Officious assumptions
Deadly dialectical deals
For many working there meals on wheels
Nepotism?
Despotism?
You said it
I felt it.

I turned on my weary heels
No one cared how it feels
Went home by bus
God help us!

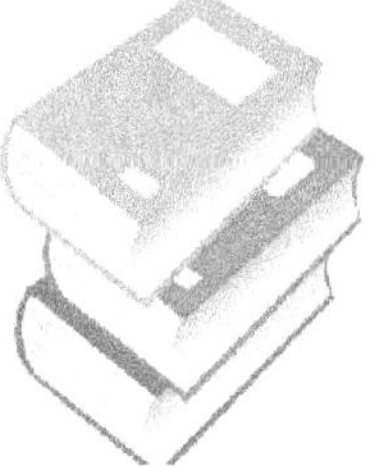

29

GOD IS LOVE

Before I sleep I play reels of the day's events
In my mind checking if everything was real
This allows me to judge and prevent,
Assuming everything is the real deal
There are so many things going on
If you don't stop to catch a breath of your own
Events will take your breath away
And you can't keep negative thoughts at bay

There's covid.
Very morbid
But even in the global chaos
We've got to ride the life chariot
That perpetual motion behemoth called life
Life must flourish for all humankind

The statistics
The tactics
Social scientists have failed
The projections even by Bill Gates hailed
Have not conformed to computer modeling
The huge gap between model and reality mind-boggling

In essence, the pandemic has taught us that
In reality, for our survival, we don't do tit for tat
Humans are the same
No need to lay blame.
A problem to one a problem to all
Even the mightiest can fall

I've got to say this again and again
Every day speaking the same refrain

30

That we need love
We need each other
That our God is the same
His power is not a political game

Those who claim to know Him
Those who think singing a Hymn
This means they are closer to God
The rest are heathens and odd
Spare us the politics
Your behaviour is apocalyptic

Our purpose here is to love
Have you shown love
Have you spread love
Do you have love
Are you in love
Are you love

If not whatever you do has nothing to do with God
God is love.
The rest is politics
Mind games
Not love
God is love

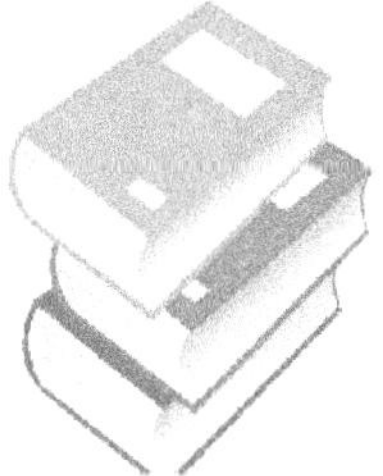

GOD IS NOT A RELIGION

God is the total of all that we see
And also what we don't see even in the sea
God is not of a certain people or any region
God is not found in human constructs such as religion
God is the energy; power and we can feel, see, hear and
smell His manifestation
God does not stoop to our misunderstanding so pray
with hesitation
God will not be found by looking up, down, below, or
above
God is love, God is love, God is love

Love yourself
Love your chef
Love the earth
Love till death it's not the end
Love everything all the time in all places
Love everyone all climes all faces all races

GOING HOME

Someone hates your personality
Two of you have no commonality
They want you to go away
Even if you want to stay
They cause a storm in your mind
Behave in many ways unkind
You have talked many a time
It's like you committed a crime
They say the room ain't big enough for both of us.
You say as you catch the next bus.

I am going home
Home where I belong
I need to sit down and think long
Sit in the garden like a gnome,
And make some resolutions
This could be a revolution
I am going, going, going home
Going, going, going home.

GREENER SCENE

Cleaner cleans river full of pollution
Greener scene on earth a revolution
This our only home
Earth our only hope
Polluter eats paper as a solution

Greener scene

Go green all over
Recycle all paper
Every plastic
Every elastic
Non-ferrous stuff
Even steel tuff
Recycle recycle
Send bicycle
Control our death
Earth is our earth
Never pollute
Every one resolute

Greener scene

We want a grinner scene. Everyone saw smiling. For that scene to be seen we need to recycle a greener scene. Don't drive to arrive, cycle that bicycle. You will be fitter and lady ozone not bitter, about how you treat her, belching stuff at her visage like a mirage in the Arabian Desert. Scientists, those pesky factual mathematically modeling fiddling meddling busybodies, have said it. The attention we haven't paid it. That energy cannot be created or destroyed but transformed

HUMAN

You may be rich preach teach or cheat
You may Burmese, Chinese, Japanese
You may be bright, white, mighty
You may be Indian, West Indian, Red Indian
You may be African, American, Jamaican
Black, white, yellow, pink, brown, or even orange

We are human
All born of woman
Covid 19 has shown us
We are on the same bus

When a person gets sick and dies
Don't ignore their misery and cries
When a person is hungry and poor
Don't ignore them and close the door
When a person different than you
Faces any challenge it is still true

We are human
All born of woman
Covid 19 has shown us
We are on the same bus
Humans are not in a special class

Human
From a woman
Be human, please do
Human be true

37

HUMANS ARE NOT IN A SPECIAL CLASS

I wanted to postulate the end
I might be there or I might not
I did this for a dear deserving friend

The topic of the end being very hot
Scriptures talk about the rapture
I have given it a lot of thought

Just as a tree dies back to nature
I believe we all join the food chain
Only the memory giving us stature.

Just as a song loses its refrain
Everything must come to pass
The memory washed away in the rain.

So I told my friend to stop being an ass
Accept we are born to die, no cry.
Humans are not in a special class.

I CAN'T COPE

This world is not my home
My thoughts not my own
Contrived, controlled

My mortgage an uncontrollable train of no gauge
Whose wheels and deals are off
Astronomic interest rates without rebates.

I need permission to breathe
Even to breed
Rulers foolers of many men

Owners of capital never capitulate
Making fresh demands for a pound of flesh
Stressing and de-stretching my life expectancy

In seven days, seven letters of demand giving seven
hours, to make good.
Though rude it is understood it's no good to even
brood.
Seven minutes and seven seconds to go to my seventh
haven, Incarceration.

Remand demands I give up all I have and behave
according to those affording me life
Like I was born without rights to fight for my plight.

Seven seconds left, I raised my eyes from the seven
writs and was amazed at the profligacy of the
bourgeoisie.

The proletariat worse

39

I AM PERFECT NOW

I could never do anything right
You always wanted me out of sight
I was even responsible for your flatulence
Even though you were ill with incontinence
Every one of your miseries
Was due to me not your usury
Even when the weather was inclement
You blamed me for your debts' increment
Now that you have caused my demise
There is nothing for you to demand
Your secret will rot with my carcass
No one will know you caused my car crash
I'm too deep to hear your thunder
I'm perfect now lying six feet under

JESUS

Last time two thousand and twenty years ago as told by Julius and Augustus Caesar, he was a cool dude doing some hippie stuff. The seers drinking holy beers saw him coming in a flying saucer all the way from heaven to appear at the Church of Jesus Christ of Latter-day Saints. The dude arrived like a wizard in a winnowing basket. The tot was already hi-tech didn't want to bother surrogate mom Mary the...Ummm....the maiden, with stuff like morning sickness, bloating, and cravings. So the kid just arrived next to Joe and old Joe's jokes became stale.

Old Joe, drank a drum of ale and had no illicit brewed ale to sell the next morn.

Cool dude didn't like his brother man tortured, abused, or robbed so with cigar and sombrero he stood his ground, hand on his point four chewing his tobacco. The sheriff didn't like him in town sent his posse and said " Room ain't big enough for the both of us". By the time robocop and batmobile came for him, the dude had skipped town on a heavenly broom but the sheriff being also the bailiff hung the wrong guy and made the wrong entry in his book to look cool to King Herod of the Julius Caesar fame.

All this poetry and stuff they wrote about dude Jesus is all for the movies and many movies now made of him when he was just the dude down the street doing good, chilling with guys and girls up to no good.

I mean turning water into wine without yeast and a brewery and turning stuff into bread to feed the hungry are guys watching too much sci-fi stuff.

I miss the dude, though, he needs to come back and we go smoke some joint and mess around like real homies do.

I HAVE SO MANY...

I have so many thoughts in my head
Some are dead
Some are sad
Some are mad
Some are good
Some are rude

I have so many sores on my body
Some are shoddy
Some are healing
Some have feeling
Some have pus
Some have gas

I have so many poems in my book
Some they spook
Some are sweet
Some a treat
Some are horror
Some an aura

I have so many friends in the world
Some are worthy
Some are steady
Some are nerdy
Some are fascist
Some are racist

I have so many things
Some are thin
Some are...
Some...

So.......
S......

I PRAY

Here I am again, Lord
On the long winding road
Doing the same old things
Sorry, to say, committing the same old sins

I have been
I have seen

Those who say Africa amounts to nothing
Now know that nothing is something

You told me to be patient
Treat them with patience
Never to gloat
Eat my goat
While they gluttonously eat caviar
Slothfully, even, in a way cavalier

You said in our Negro culture
We are not a vulture
We do not profit from the misfortune
We spend estate and fortune
Helping those unfortunate
The rich Fortune 500 magnate
be they delusionally obstinate
We love, even, the obdurate

We love all

45

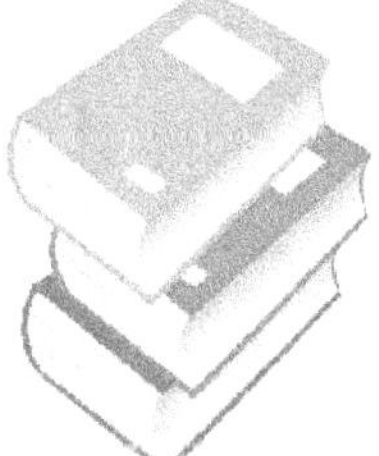

When they fall
Forgive them, Father
Teach them rather
That what You the Father of All
What you create will stand tall
Till you recall
In winter or fall

No one renders asunder
With bombs and thunder
That which you're breathing doth give
And gave the grace to live

It's true
It's You
Omnipotent
Omnipresent
Our omnibus
Our Omni-love

You know what else burdens your creation
You know I seek to love, commune, and recreation

Let my spirit speak to you
Let your Godliness come through
And forgive
Pardon, give
Those who denigrate your Negro Child
Using graphic imagery going wild

46

We love them
Our love game
Your name
The same

Grant them your grace and contritional atonement
To their no conditional atonement
Heal the sick
DON-T, pick

Forgive
Let live
I say
I pray

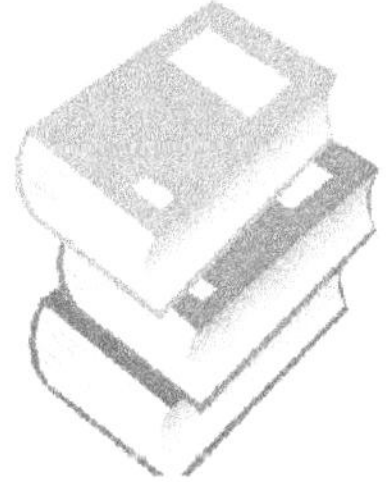

JUST A WORD

Come travel with me in this travail

This life, let's unravel its mystery without trammel

Driven by the marvelous desire of a traveler,

With unrivalled passion to unravel,

Without drivel, the ravenous ditties of life unlimited.

Let's marvel at the superfluity of what constitutes the navel of our existence and discover that it's all just poetic justice. We shall reveal in the sumptuous delicacy of our poetry and thereon come to understand why everything, in the beginning, is just a word. That's it. Just a word.

JUST THE THREE OF US

I walked alone before now
I did not like to bow
I was sure of the purpose
Sure of my course
So I thought
But my life was fraught
Unending controversy
Justice a travesty

I sought some help
I was still at the helm
But I would bow my head
And ask to go ahead
My fortunes improved
And this to be proved
I should never go alone
If an unsure stay at home

In moments of many minds
Faced with life's little binds
I realized I need assistance
Now I consult in every instance
And go forth wearing a shield
I go confidently into any field,
With God and his Son
Just the three of us.
Longing to be heard

I sit down and listen all day
They think I have nothing to say hi
Like only they can pray
I nod my head in fake acquiescence

LONGING TO BE HEARD

The men say because I am a female
I am not allowed to speak at sermons
I know their pastor is a shemale
They ignore me for their acquaintance, but I'm longing
to be heard

I see the young adolescents waiting
The teenage boy misunderstood paining
My grandparents' old fashioned straining
Husband, wife, girl or boyfriend, everyone,
Longing to be heard

Someone listen before it's too late
Unlessening has sealed many a fate

LOST CAUSE

Guy without cause lost pose because of those
Those in who powerful power repose
Tried a coup the cost
Tried campaign he lost
Worked for the one he had tried to depose

Lost cause

A man lost his pose because of his girth
His friends always laughed at him since birth
At the annual contest (he was an alien)for refugees
He decided to submit a portrait of his effigy.

Lost cause

L-osing is part of winning
O-ne wins due to scheming
S-hame befalls the loser
T-he loser the accuser
C-ausing embarrassment

A-ccusing winner of embezzlement
U-ntil people get tired of the circus
S-illy accusations of hocus pocus
E-very loser knows it's a lost cause

SO LOVE COMES IN MANY COLOURS

Love can be sweeter
Or it can also be bitter
Verily, it can make you crazy
Even sometimes it's hazy
Combined sugar, salt, and vinegar
Oh yes, you can fall with vigour
Many times not sure you're in out
Every day wishing you lived without
So many sides to the game of love
In love, you go and you come
Not sure whether to commit
Many times sending a committee
And making the situation worse
Not all saying the right words
You realize it has many colours
Colours as many as flowers
Orange is sweet and bitterish
Love can be blue and bickerish
Oh, sometimes green with envy
Undercurrents due to poison ivy
Red splatter for star crossed lovers
So love comes in many colours

LOVE

Love?
What is it?
Is this it?
Love is an enigma
You can ask your ma
Is it even something?
Or is it nothing?
Is it tangible?
Tangy? Edible?

Love can make you well
Been in love you can easily tell
But, it can also make you unwell
And can make someone swell
Even sick
Lovesick
Missing chick
Her tricks
You stop to think
Act thick

Love can be pure pleasure
You give away treasure
In large measure
To enjoy the leisure
Of being in love
Of having a home
You are welcome
You feel wholesome

Love can be a real pain
Driving you insane

53

Pain all over
Whether young or older
Pain in the head
A headache you dread
Pain in the heart
Can send you away in a hearse
Pain in the back
You feel like you want to backtrack
Pain here
Pain there
Everywhere pain pain
Pain pain

There are as many types of love
As there are infinite stars above
The love of "any" different from "one"
The love of "many" different from "hon"
The love of God is unique
Different than the love of gold and Monique
The love of country
The love of pantry
Love of a hobby you enjoy
Different than a love of envoy

So what is love; you ask?
That one is a hard task
Suffice it to say
Just for today
Love is what it is
It is what you make it
Love someone
Love something
Love nothing
Love yourself

54

It's still love
Love?
Yes love
Love

It's still love
Love?

LIMERICKALLY ACROSTICALLY SERIOUSLY JOKER

My bossy boss is not amused. She says "These love poems of yours..umm....are you alright? ". So I am like blushing, but my skin is so dark. Thank God for it's not noticeable. "Are you cheating on me? ! ".

So I have been at great pains to explain that poetry is not necessarily about reality but about exploring novel ways of saying something with the greatest impact. I am not sure she believes me but I am under reconnaissance from "The Spy Who Loves Me"...this one not undercover....well, sometimes undercover. Pun intended.

So what does a smart alleck poet like DM do? He does the deed in a different way to avoid being locked up in a love quarantine. I write poems in a limerickally acrostically seriously joking manner. That ought to keep my bossy boss in the kitchen...where all beautiful women belong. I joke! Women belong on PH cryyyyying their hearts out about men and men belong on mars with scars their cars among the stars...

As usual, if you believe all this you need to have your head gasket checked. Peace out.

LONG SILENT NIGHT

Lonely moments are a rare treat
One gets to talk to himself in silence
No one around to shatter your peace
Good to see the cold winter gone
Summer is here with me as promised
I spend the day in the company of the sun
Long shadows my only company
Enveloped in a cocoon of private thoughts
No one at home except my dog and cat
The wife and grown kids gone visiting
Now the sun is bidding me good night
In comes a more intimate silence
Good for searching the soul alone
High on my mind is to write a poem
The poem about a Long Silent Night.

MAKE-BELIEVE

It's nice to believe in miracles
To spend the day with the oracle
It's nice to believe in angels
To read the bible from all angles
It's nice to think you have a special power
To think any bush is a special flower

It's bad to believe in the occult
To belong to a dangerous cult
It's bad to wish someone harm
To blackmail and twist their arm
It's bad to believe in pure fiction
To do things to cause affliction

The weird world of make-believe
The world of make-believe
Make-believe

Only Science works,
Science with Technology
Science with Engineering
Science with Mathematics

Leave the world of make-believe
The world of make-believe
STEM the tide stop the slide

MR. CONTROVERSY

Mr. Controversy, Mr. Controversy, Sir
Do you remember the trouble you stirred
When others wanted to go right
You decided to go left and fight,
The mob psychology that goes with groups
Of course, some thought you wanted a coup

Mr. Controversy, Mr. Controversy, hey!
Do you remember from your teenage day
Others did Sankukai and Shukokai too
You went on your own did Jeet Kune Do
Do you remember when you became Headboy
In secondary school, you refused to be anybody's toy

Mr. Controversy, Mr. Controversy, Mister
Do you remember running for office, a minister
Not once but twice you were treated like a fool
Then at the farm, they voted for you
In your absence your actions they knew
Wherever you go whatever you do its true

Mr. Controversy, such is your life
Just hide yourself in a poem and continue to rhyme.

MY BRAIN TELLS ME THIS, MY HEART THAT, MY SOUL THE ARBITER

My brain tells me this, my heart that, my soul the
arbiter
My soul takes over when my heart, the shrew, argues
with its crew, my brain
Oft times my heart wants despite the risk, my brain
counsels caution
Disagreements vicious, I end up in depression, my heart
in a tantrum.

My soul takes over when my heart, the shrew, argues
with its crew, my brain.
I meditate in conversation with my soul, the arbiter
Disagreements vicious, I end up in depression, my heart
in a tantrum.
My soul asks, 'Would you wish it upon yourself'; the
issue is settled.

I meditate in conversation with my soul, the arbiter.
Oft times my heart wants, despite the risk, my brain
counsels caution.
My soul asks, 'Would you wish it upon yourself'; the
issue is settled.
My brain tells me this, my heart that, my soul the
arbiter.

MY EXISTENCE

My little dot in the universe is here constructed in
verses
Non-existent in the multiverse
Infinitesimally small
Even in my nothingness, I walk tall
Knowing my relative nanometric none existence is Love
Love is huge as it comes
Holding everything in mathematical wonder
Nothing is a blunder

So tell me which mad Adventist
An adventurist
Comes with scurvy
In abject retrogression, a navy
Nervy
And envy
To tell me it's not my spot
Not my dot.
Blacked out
In my black hole, I shout

'Let me be'
'I want to be me'
'Look see'
'I want to be free'

My little dot in the universe is here constructed in
verses
Non-existent in the multiverse
Infinitesimally small
Even in my nothingness, I walk tall

With these little verses
No one reverses
My existence
My existence insistence.

A HORSE

If wishes were horses then I would wish I had a horse
I would sing for it till my voice was hoarse
I would do it with watery leather
To ride the world in all its weather
My horse would earn me money at the races
Take me to church the pub and all places
With my horse, we would do heists
Rob the rich to give poor the poorest the highest
With my horse, I would amass wealth
Ride to the alchemist when in poor health
I would not want for food
I would go rob Robin Hood
Let him do all the noble dirty work
Then ride up to him take all his sweat
I would ride to find King Solomon's mine
The mythical mine in Zimbabwe going past the River
Rhine
My horse I would take to the magic forest
Have a wizard fit turbo wings so that there be no need
for rest
I would burgle cases and cases of Red Bull
To make sure my wings are also cool
Then we would ride over the oceans looking for a
maiden
For me a fresh young lady, for my horse a filly to carry
its burden
Over the Atlantic to Brazil to sample a Samba Dancer
North we would gallop and fly to Mexico to avoid
prostate cancer
Onward to North America to Sin City

Quickly move on before a cop fired a round at my horse
settee
In Europe, I would go to Holland
To the red lights districts, the whore land
There only for a short time
Coz my horse in street a serious crime
I would fly to Russia, not for long, being too cold
The Tsar, my friend, being too old
Gallop passed China away from Corona
On to India where the cows have no COWrona
Then fly back to Zimbabwe to marry, again, my wife
My horse being tired and worn out I would retire for life
Oh, I wish I had a horse I called Wish
My life would be so good and so sweet.

MY HOUSE

I love my house.
It ain't no castle but it's got a few love tricks up its
rooms to make Windsor swoon with jealousy.
Make no mistake my house boss wears a blouse and a
mercurial attitude to boot.
I have tried to be mainly about the house but end up in
a skirt with lots of eggs on my face.

My house has a couple of rooms enough to keep
another couple or two in a private embrace but a
couple of fights and beef has made me realize there can
be only one couple with one boss. My couple and one
beautifully mean, I mean, bossy boss I shall not want.
She makes me down to lie and sometimes to lie to save
the peace, in duvets of all colours even when I am not
feeling sleepy. But I digress.

We were talking about the house and not the boss.

Three bedrooms, separate WC and shower/tub, a
pantry leading to a pesky kitchen which is never big
enough for the boss. Aah, the boss again!

A living room, a lounge, and a patio. From the lounge,
you sneak into the biggest worse, and most action-filled
secret wonderland in the manor...the bedroom. Don't
get ideas yet. More of what really happens in there in a
moment. No guessing. Then outside space for my three
chariots and my Maltese dogs Ziggy and Flossy. Not to
forget my wily sly feline bundle of amazing grace.

MY CAT

That's my house. You wanna know more, stick around
when we do a sequel to the most luscious hardworking,
and kindest boss ever. Never a dull moment at my
house.
My life with my wife

I like my life with my wife because it's quite nice.
We have been seen together since her teen when she
was fifteen
It is fair to say we have been there for so long it's rare
I hope we continue to cope and be on top of the
troubles of the globe
To be frank I thank my wife, my friend her loving spirits
never sank
Come what may, may love grace our home on and on
and on.

MY WORD

If I die
Don't cry
When I die
Don't lie
How I die
Don' ask why
Time I die
Don't sigh
Why I die
Don't pry

Am here
No fear
Of death
On earth
I die
I try
To renew
Anew
My word
In world

My work
My word
Will live
Will give
The world
My worth
Alive
Alike
Or dead
Instead.

67

NOTHING

Today's poem is of nothingness. Absolutely nothing. The poem is not
Political, not religious, not racist, not nihilistic, not even chauvinist. It is not even about tribalism or any of the political isms; socialism, Nazism, or capitalism. Nor about Black Lives Matter, White Lives Matter, or All Lives Matter.

This poem is about nothing. It is saying nothing. Only that it's a poem saying nothing. That is to say of nothingness. They say if you have nothing to say don't say it. Since I have nothing to say this is why I am saying nothing through this poem of nothingness.

Remember that in the beginning there was nothing. Only the Word was there. This poem, though saying nothing, has a lot of words. So the poem is also nothing with a lot of words. It is therefore possible that this poem of nothing will create something since it has lots of words. The words of this nothingness poem might create a poem. Or a rhyme. It Maybe a limerick

Today is the day with nothing to say
In the beginning, I say when I pray,
The Word was there
Then there was air
Wordy Limerick poem might create clay

OH...

An angelic face
Handsome even
Contours in harmony with forehead
Cheekbones GB complementary to a nose bereft of
haughtiness.

Draped in simple but laundered apparel. Handy helpful
hands from sleeves made of silk. Hands holding a New
Testament, itself a testament to a man of the cloth.

Tongue speaking in tongues; of love, brotherhood, and
the promise of eternal life. An honourable man.

Oh, hail him!

Till you have the fortunate misfortune of looking behind
him. His flip side. A cudgel in his left hand dripping
innocent blood.

Raw diamonds in pockets were confiscated from
scrawny artisanal miners.
Gold teeth-replacing rotten canines in a fouled-up
mouth.
In his right-hand fake writs of execution in a foreign
language.

Feet with boots of brutality stained with the blood of
slave labourers
Scarred with hate for anyone and everything breathing,
let alone breeding.

Oh, hell him!

69

ODE TO UNKNOWN POETS

They say I am now number one
On PH where I came to have fun
For me, it's not about the numbers
Focusing on numbers encumbers
Makes a poet write for the sake of writing
Instead of posting for the sake of poeting

I don't even know where to check rankings
I don't even know who to give thankings
For reviewing poems and ranking
For reading reggae poems and skanking
At my age, some things are not important
At my age some times I am impotent

In my life, I am used to controversy
Most times, not my fault just a travesty
I like to express myself to the fullest
To others, this is not really the coolest
But isn't this what makes it lively and strong?
As long as I don't insult someone am not wrong.

To my haters, I say I love you so
To my friends, I love you even more
Don't worry about rankings oh no
Worry about writing poems you know
Till we meet in metaphoric imagery
Happy poeting ignore conflicts imaginarily

70

ON AND ON AND ON

A lone forlorn man got on the phone alone
Frozen to the bone his tone like a stone
He overslept
His phone he kept
"Mayday! Mayday! " He mourned in the storm

On and on and on

Tom got stoned missed the lone plane
He played Simon and Garfunkel's' song to remain sane
"To get your plane right on time"
He played it on and on and on into the night

On and on and on

O-ne day the Corona Virus will be gone
N-ormalcy returns no need to be alone
A-ll people of the world will celebrate
N-ewly weds no longer celibate
D-eath will recede to the dungeon
O-nly happy people will club on
N-o longer afraid to hug and kiss
A-ll embracing those they missed
N-ow the question will be asked
D-epartments of sociology tasked
O-ne question to ask on the phone
N-ext time do people know how to

Love and live on and on and on?

71

PIETY

Every twinkling star a sun like ours
Burning light for millions of hours
Trillions of sparkling diamonds
Some shaped like almonds
To every star are worlds, some cold
Some made seconds ago, some old
Others temperate and hot
Some habitable, some not
Earth minuscule
Belief in a fiat
Religion a ridicule
Piety.
Religion is war
Each claiming to be IT,
causing intolerance the more,
Not accommodating a bit.
Science says we are the same,
But religion has a chosen race,
Calling messiahs by name,
Even conjuring up a face.
We must foster human friendship,
Spend time and money on science, building a spaceship,
Instead of suffering the mind games in silence.

THE PROJECT NOT TAKEN

I am a dreamer, a joker, and a poet
So, I thought we could use a poem
The satirical one about myself
"One two three" now it's on the shelf
Buddy bard friends not interested
All my poetic juices sequestrated
I guess people are different
Some are rigid and indifferent
Here in Africa, we have fun
Any excuse we go play in the sun
A group comes together
There is singing, dancing forever
Endowed women shaking assets
Not standing there like Fred Basset

Men hounding them around
Drums beating hands pounding
Stomping feet, jumping sky high
Nubile girls to boys saying "Hie"
A fire, a braai with delicious meat
A carnival right down the street
Covid forgotten
Police rotten
Army in fatigue
Quite an intrigue
Everywhere people working to a frenzy
The bourgeois class in flashy Benzie's
Tempo rising
People fighting
Blood flowing all over
Army in Land Rovers
Beautiful scenery

73

Not like Sean Connery

Cut!
And cut!

Title adapted from Robert Frost's "The road not taken".
Credits due.

YOU CAN'T COME OUT OF LIFE ALIVE

You can't come out of life alive
That's why every moment is precious
Do not capitulate to anyone
Your human rights are supreme
Even if they murder you coldly
Die peacefully and boldly
The living will continue the fight
And the future will be put right

PICKET FENCE

Meet me at the picket fence
Each stands a metre or two apart
That's our first line of defense
We can no longer share a tart

We used to have breakfast
On your loan or mine
Now we don't know can we outlast
This lockdown quagmire

Neighbour did you wash your hands
Did you sanitize
Before you came to the picket fence
Do you realize...

We can only meet at the picket fence
Our line of defense
The picket fence
In this Covid offense

PERILOUS PAYLOAD

In your mind a war brews
Protagonists in your mind
Battlefield in your mind
Cassius belli in your mind

The sun rises every day smiling
The moon chasing the sun grinning
The wind sings verses in trees
The chorus by the gumtrees

But there is no ceasefire in your head
The battle is a heavy load
On a lonely winding road
With a spiritual payload.

A perilous payload
Lord unload the perilous payload
The perilous payload
Perilous payload

PERIODIC FABLE

I want to tell you a periodic fable
Based on the periodic table
Some elements are very stable
Like salt garnishing food on the table
Never mind sodium married chlorine
Some chemicals will cause cholic
Some elements are unstable even volatile
Hydrocarbons for fuel taking you many miles
Each element on the periodic table has its own use
Even if we discard it in the refuse

Every human is an important element
There is no need for racial enmity
The best, most stable people are mixed race
Genetic diversity making them strong with a pretty face
Some think tribal purity is important
Brothers marry sisters leading to impotence
Oxygen marrying oxygen to form air
It takes hydrogen for water to be there
To some, this periodic fable may read strange
But rules of nature never change.

PINK PURPLISH ROSE

My pink purplish rose
Let me rest my weary head in your petals
Immerse my sensory nerves in your nectar
The friendly bee buzzing sonnets
Lullabies for our progeny
Drinking off of your sweet nectar
Rewarding us with life-giving gonads
Hardworking nomads
At the break of dawn, you open for me
To bask in radiance, to the symphony of tweeting little
birds
By nightfall, you cover me softly with a natural essence.
My pink purplish rose.

PLASTIC PEOPLE

Governments have been banning, unbanning
The environment has been dying, undying
Screaming in abject pain
The rain washing it plain
Streaming in every stream
It's everywhere on earth choking us to death
In the air and our lungs
In our hair and our aqualungs
In the water, we drink
The pipes of the sink
Your pocket for your shopping,
The rocket for planet-hopping
Your food
Any good?
Your car
Take you far?
Andy and Mandy
Sandy and Randy
Every human being Smile,
Every smile for miles,
It's plastic.

PLEASURE PAIN DARKNESS LIGHT

Occurrences unnatural
Response irrational
The pleasure of pain
Driving you insane
No explanation
No exclamation?

In the darkness there's light
Imagination taking flight
What if the sun never shone?
In the darkness, you're not alone
An abnormality
A normality?

The pleasure of pain in light of darkness
An abnormality a normality
No explanation no exclamation
"A natural mystic in the air"
Pleasure pain darkness light
Pleasure
Pain
Darkness
 Light

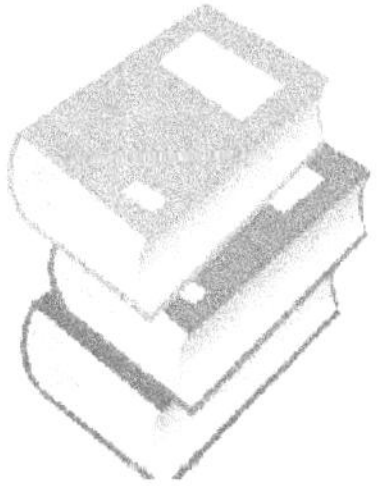

POOR LOVER'S TIME

A flower towered over the power line
Lovers cowered undercover doing fine
Time was standing still
Thieves live cables steal
Electric shocks soured poor lover's time

Poor lover's time

P-rivacy is supreme
O-nly for two beings
O-nly for lovers
R-etreat under covers
L-ocked in embrace
O-pen dress
V-ery intimate
E-ven private
R-espect them
S-ay to them damn
T-ake cover
I-n your lover
M-ost times
E-veryone having a poor lover's time

Poor lover's time.

It hurts so so bad when you love someone
For some reason, they can't or won't love you back
The feelings of rejection are devastating to everyone
Ignoring these love rejection feelings is a big mistake
It's a universal truth
Love brings forth fruit
Without love there is nothing

Nothing at all to call something
If you are bereft of love in all its manifestations
In all its impetuous impulsivity and hesitations
You are nothing
Not worth a farthing
You can cry
Die
Try
Lie
Sigh
No one cares
No one dares

So we must all find love
Let the power of love come
In the home
In the dome
In church
We search
Underseas
Overseas
In all continents
Love commitments
In America
In Africa
South America
North America
Southeast Asia
Minor and Major Asia
The Middle East
The Dragon east
We must find love so fine
Even in poor lover's time

83

Without loving something
There's nothing
Nothing.

POEM FOR THE POET

Do not ye run out of things to write,
Pour your feelings out even if it sounds trite
Yours is to gab when the rest have gone silent
Yours is to grab attention with ideas even salient
Do not ye forget whither the ink and pen
Scour your mind with wormy words like a hungry hen
Yours is to shout loudly without opening your mouth
Yours is to speak truth to power till they go south
Do not be averse to talk to that thesaurus,
Words and rhymes never extinct like the dinosaurs
Yours is to bring forth tears coated
In words
Yours is to bring ideas from earth's other worlds
Do not be averse to sit in solitude in the bush
Snakes, flying insects, and bitey ants will be like "shush!
",
Give you a wide berth knowing it's your alone time
For, you are a poet, the primer of the primeval rhyme
The persistent writer of what others do not say
This is the Poem for the Poet for today.

POEM OF SADNESS

I wanna do a poem of sadness
Today to show my madness
My heartstrings all detuned sadly
Playing a discordant arpeggio badly
Blues songs in a medley
Depressing spirit steadily
I look around me
Breathe the air free
I say to myself
"You blood elf! "

Some are dying
Some are crying
You've got your life
Having things nice
A home
A phone
A farm
A barn
Cars
No scars

My poem of sadness
Is a poem of gladness

POEMS EVERYWHERE

My home is a happy home
It is clad in poems all over
On the roof are little birds
Singing sweet sonnets
A discordant raven hops about
Pecking on wriggling worms
To the rhythm of their cawing
Hop skip jump caw caw caw
My cat feigns disinterest
Biding its time to pounce
Ziggy my Maltese is smitten.
Flossy the bitch on heat
The best poetry is in my poultry
The cacophony of mother hens
Tending to their hen chicks
My home is a happy home
The mother of the house, mom
Makes sure there's peace and harmony
No one, to her family, brings harm on
And, my job is simple enough
To make sure I see poems everywhere.

And I see poems everywhere.
Poems everywhere.

POET DIAL HER MA

To write a poem or not to write
To rhyme couplets or just be trite
To write in prose or to write a sonnet
The miss in a sun hat or a bonnet
Is it a lyric or in the mood for a limerick
To write a ballad about a damsel with a malady
Or free verse maybe with many a reverb
Poets dilemma she needs to dial her ma.
Poet oh poet

Poet oh poet my buddy bard
Must you stoop so low as to judge the poet?
Poems must come with different messages
Some deep, some light, some downright anti-
establishment
Some irreverent, some political, some playful, and some
joyful.
The poet is a messenger.
Judge the poem, not the poet. There are things you
don't know.
Unless you are just a *#-+:; ! ! Poet.

POET AND POETESS

Poet; listen and listen well
This may sound rude
If you love that lass
Don't go telling us
We couldn't care less
We don't care about your fuss
Show us how you love her
So we know love is the air
What are you willing to give?
Your life, your house, or a shirt without a sleeve

Poetess hear me well
Your poetic desire you want to quell
You found a nice handsome man
We don't care his name is Stan
Take him apart for me
Let me see how he measures up to be
A good man or just a Casanova
How does he get you to the supernova
Does he snore like a volcano
Or is he rigid in ways like a mechano

There are waterfalls to fall over
The galaxy to take the moon rover
The sun an easy friendly target
The faithful moon smiling like Margret
The wind, the water, and the earth
Fun Scooby-Doo cartoons for your mirth
Poetess and poet my companions
Make us join you in your poetic opinions
By tickling our imagination with metaphors
Feed us rhymes like ruminants and herbivores.

RAIN RAIN RAIN

I see the rain falling
We have been forever calling
For an end to this cruel drought
People and animals food without
Our farming economy sliding,
Backward mothers and children crying

A farmer's blood on the boil
Eager to plow and work the soil
It's been three long painful years
Nation shedding crocodile tears
People struggling and starving
Donor vultures divisions causing
Trying to influence the nation
With a tainted donor ration

We are not lazy people
We are not loafers or feeble
Like everywhere else on earth
Global warming causing death
Then adding salt to injury, Covid!
All over the world situation morbid

In the middle of abject despair
The human soul in disrepair
God is having a serious conversation
With His creation, is my observation
Some were wearing His shoes
Not knowing the size of His shoe will contuse
As Jesus said "Give to Caesar what belongs to Caesar"
So shall it be? Be warned of all who play God. Cease it!
Aah! !!

I am not into religion, God forbid!
Religion achieving nothing concrete
But I see God everywhere
Omnipresent but nowhere
In my home
When I am alone
In other humans
Male, female, or the Shoeman

Rain clouds rain rain rain
Wash away our life strain
Wring cumulonimbus dry
Let the heavens let loose and cry
Embarrass them who are sly
Profiting from those in drought die
Instead of spreading the love of God
Siphoning our diamonds and gold
Priests and perverts

Sorry, Molly, for the horror story
Gory trolling in lorry of glory
Not photography
But pornography
Priests and perverts in the same space are folly

PRIESTS AND PERVERTS

Priests hate trysts
Revile what we try-eth
In their mind that is sin
Eve having done the thing
Some say so in public
Try things a bit oblique
Soon as they are alone
And then confess to atone
Nature made us what we are
Despite doctrines not getting us far
Priests insist on celibacy in faith
Even use Mary the Virgin's face
Remember we can't fight nature
Verily, I say, nature will nurture,
Every person provided we obey it
Remain on this earth and be fit
To all human beings, I implore I imply
Sorry, ignore this, go forth and multiply

POETRY BUS

The way things are
I am going far
I am taking a hike
On my bike
Going somewhere
Don't know where
Where to go
Where they won't say no
On the basis of belief
Belief is no relief

Here in my county
In my country
They believe we are fine
It's a matter of time
Before we implode
Things explode
I have got to hit the tar
Go away far
In my mind
On the rebound

I never run
I love my fun
My people
Looking through the peephole
Of our history
The mystery
But the way thus far
Wearing my scar
I need to leave
On my poetry bus, I shall live

93

POETRY, ME AND FREEDOM

I am not alone in my life
I have siblings, kids, and a wife
Even so, I walk alone in the wilderness of my mind. From birth, I have been trudging the interminable path to nowhere. I'm not even sure whether I go. The path meanders down vertical cliffs, worm-infested swamps, viper-ruled jungles, and even deserts without an oasis. All in my mind. I trudge on to find solace. The only place I am free. The only place I can be me. That place is poetry. With poetry, I arrive.

They told me to be an engineering professional.
To study hard and be a professor.
So, I wasted my life with Pythagoras, La Place, Isaac Newton, and Albert Einstein. Kudos to these big minds, but they have brought more rumination and misery to my mind. Their complicated equations dulled my eloquence. Melted my synapses where verbal acuity resides. I should have sparred with William Shakespeare in metaphor without shaking the spear. I should have polished his shoes and helped to feed cannabis in his pipe. I should have jousted with Achinua Achebe and learned his literary aptitude. I should have helped Achebe educate Africa so that things don't fall apart. In their scholastic virtuosity lies my psychedelic consummation. Pure ecstasy. My solace. The only place I can be me. That place in poetry. With poetry, I arrive.

They say "In the beginning was the Word"
The word creates and influences the world. My restlessness stems from not having the Word. The wherewithal to wield it to maximum effect. I will never be like the poets of yore or the great contemporary writers and scribes, but I can write my mind. For, when I try to speak, no one listens. I try to write, no one reads. I try to protest, they say I am a rebel. I try to explain, they shout me down. I found the keys. The keys of freedom. I have found my solace. The only place I can be me. That place is poetry. With poetry, I arrive.

READER?

You can do a wondrously wonderful poem
Wonderfully winding in the poetic wind, winding, finding it grinding, binding, and extending its whole worth over the world. It's Woolworth in the cold. Called and sold in the folds of your mould. The whole world enthralled in the workings of its metaphors, the imaginary, images emerging, merging in the verges of your Shakespearean subconscious. That your organic antennaic protrusion resplendent in your cranial medulla oblongata. Nay, you can rise with the prose to great heights. You can mourn, sob, wail, and fail to control your emotion, Lord! ..The commotion in the locomotion in your location.

God forbid! That's morbid! Worse than Covid! How sordid! Even torrid!

A poet has written that once in a lifetime poem.
The one that causes the bard the tears to pour 'em.

ALAS!

A POEM BECOMES A POEM WHEN IT FINDS A READER

Please people on PH
Forget ph on PH
Read poems
Reader read this feed.
Reader?

A REBEL'S REFRAIN

I don't just get on the train
I wanna find out its true destination
How long it will stop at the station
The weather whether it will rain
The speed will travel
All these questions I unravel
And I maintain
A rebel's refrain

There say there is a religion
To the facts
They lack tact
A religion without a region
They say this is the only way
For my future, I have to pray
I retain
A rebel's refrain

They say this is the convention
If you put to the test
You discard the rest
It's not supported by the observation
Do it anyway just because
I don't just follow a cause
In me remains
A rebel's refrain

So you can preach teach scream screech till the end of
time
You can threaten act certain maintain iron curtain
You can wave your figures act bigger finger on the
trigger

97

You can sanction take action give reaction wrought
destruction
Know that I shall ask if the task you assign is not a sign
of madness
Know that I shall quip if the equipment
You give me won't cause sadness
I always entertain
A rebel's refrain

REBEL MOVEMENT

A rebel rebels against a government
His military rank high in the movement
He is a good man
He's facing a ban
The problem he wants more tea improvement

Rebel movement

R-epeating the same script
E-very time wealth in a pit
B-e ready to hear about rebels
E-conomic benefit trebles
L-ook at Mozambique now
M-ore oil more trouble how
O-il and aluminum bonanza
V-iolence starting like a stanza
E-conomic benefit for foreigners
M-ozambiqueans to the coroner
E-very time in Africa and Yemen
N-ever the capitalist ever learning
T-o change the cruel script yearly

Rebel movement

1.

The old script scripted to shift attention from massive
resource looting oil majors colluding and concluding
that deluding people who are feeble keep them fighting
while siphoning riches reaching trillions again forgetting
God is there and watching.

2.

Remember Libya's richest, fittest, cutest life, better than so-called first-world countries full of counties with mounties looking for foreign bounties. They came they saw they know not peace while black gold flows to foreign auction floors sinking stowaways on the ocean floor again forgetting God is there and watching.

3.

In the house of stone, an oil found flowing glowing the same oil majors knowing leader kowtowing to be called darling to the snarling knurling head of the beast to the detriment of countrymen and infantrymen hobnobbing with pure evil selling soul all to highest bidder feeder of misery in usury and again forgetting God is there and watching.

RESURRECTION?

Five thousand and twenty years ago
Horus was born of the Virgin Iris
Born on 25th of December
Three Wise Men were led by the Eastern star to his
birth

Escaped to Egypt to escape Typhon who wanted him
killed
Was taught in a temple as a child
Baptized by Anup the Baptizer at thirty
Had twelve disciples

Did miracles and walked on water
Raised El-Azureus from the dead
Transfigured on a mount
Was crucified on a cross and resurrected from the dead

He was given the following titles
The Son of Man, the Messiah, the Word, the way, the
truth, and the light, God's anointed Son, the morning
star, the good shepherd, the lamb of the world.

Two thousand and twenty years ago
Jesus was born of the Virgin Mary
Three Wise Men were led by the Northern star to his
birth

Escaped to Egypt to escape Herod who wanted him
killed
He was taught in a temple as a child
Baptized by John the Baptist at thirty
Had twelve disciples

101

Did miracles including walking on water
Raised Lazarus from the dead
Was transfigured on a mount
Was crucified on a cross and resurrected from the dead

He was given the following titles
The Son of Man, the Messiah, the Word, the way, the
truth, and the light, God's anointed Son, the morning
star, the good shepherd, the lamb of the world.

Resurrection?

RIGHT TURN

Right turn

Spurn evil burn the urn idol turn right
Furnish your soul with armor for the fight
The devil is real
Your soul he will steal
Church in Churchill Avenue has the light

RIGHT TURN

R-est assured that the Creator
I-s there will never leave you in a crater
G-o to Him for all your salvation
H-e will love you for your devotion
T'rust Him with your whole being
T-rust Him to wash away your sin
U-ndo the scars from faithlessness
Remember He just wants truthfulness
N-o retreat no surrender turn right

103

RHYTHM CONFESSIONS

I will redeem my poetry
My Rhythm Confessions
I will try not to rhyme
I will cry in abject pain
I am so used to couplets
I am so abused by poetic sound

Makes me sick
Takes me time to heal
Like the heart of a jilted lover
Like a part of my poetry infected
Bad is the day self-expression dies
Sad is the way people judge you
As if judgment day isn't coming
At least I should be free a bird in a tree till the day

I am choking
I am smoking in my brain
A clutch on a steep slope
As such labouring
Not to rhyme
Hot is my soul
I ask my spirit
Task my telepathy
It says it's busy
It pays to be patient

'Please try again later'
'The number you dialed is not available'

I wait in the morning
I wait in the afternoon

104

I wait at night
I am still waiting
I am, till eternity
To redeem myself
My Rhythm Confessions

ROAD TO DAMASCUS IN POESY

How was I supposed to know that I am a poet?
Am I even a poet?
Just because I fluked a few comical words to make
someone smile?
Does that make me a poet?
In fact, what is a poet?

I went to varsity to get a degree
To try to control the elusive electron
Hopefully for the benefit of mankind
They call me an Electrical Engineer
That I earned and accepted loud and clear

I have been seriously writing whatever since two
thousand
My wife jokes that I can never cheat on her
I write my thoughts all over without even realizing it
So she just has to read bits and bits pieces to know
Whatsapp
I wonder is this a personality defect or what's up?

So I write when I am hurt
I write even before I blurt
I write when I am frustrated
Of course, I will write when and if I'm castrated
I write when I am happy and sad
I write when I am mad
I write
Even when I am not right I write

When I was ten years old cupid hit my heart hard
Puppy love got me wallowing in mud

106

Even today I remember my first "love" and my wife read
about her too
I was so smitten I wrote her name over my mum's
cardboard washing basket.
My mom understood and didn't tell dad the
troublemaker

Then in about July, I started posting on PoemHunter
I didn't know whether this is poetry or not
Whether it was lukewarm or hot
Now two poems on Member Poem of the Day
The gods must have lost their marbles
Do people actually think my raving and ranting are
marvels?

It is important in life to keep alive
You never know where you will arrive
On this life journey to Damascus
Road to Damascus in poesy

107

ROSE

Beautiful, brilliant
Refreshing, captivating, decorating
Variety, bouquet, garden, wedding
Tantalizing, relaxing, calming
Colour, aroma
Flower

A ROSE IN PROSE

True to form and not conforming to a norm
I promised to write about inanimate life forms
I wanna write a poem about a rose
Turning its life cycle into prose
As far as I know, a rose must have started as a seed
But I have never seen a seed just a stem in the weed
Stem or seed a rose by any way of growth will grow as
sweet
This I can vouch for even by way of a tweet.

What's the difference between a rose and me?
First, we are similar because we are both sweet
A rose needs water I need water too to grow
I need food a rose needs nutrients like me I know
A rose grows in situ while I can be mobile soon as I
crawl
I need to find a mate as soon as my hormones brawl
A rose just needs a bee to send gonads to another rose
If my offspring be a pretty girl I can call her Rose

They say the difference between me and a rose
We are we and roses we say they are those
They say I have a soul and a rose not at all
I beg to differ though
I have never seen my soul for real
They say it's something you feel
So therefore it is possible a rose does have a spirit
But humans don't know it that's why we kill it.

109

ROSES ARE RED, VIOLET IS MY MOTHER

I was born in a quagmire
My youth days nothing to admire
Sleeping in cattle kraals
A rebel without a cause
Walking barefoot to school
Used by all as a tool
She arrived from nowhere
Said we were going somewhere
Roses are red
Violet is my mother

She took me to a foreign land
Holding me by my hand
Found sisters to fight with
Brothers to play at will
Showed me, my real father
Put me in a good school
So I didn't end up a fool
She gave me a new life
Far far away from strife
Roses are red
Violet is my mother

She showed me, my real mother
Said I was born like any other
Sent me to the best school
Gave me the right tools
To stand for my convictions

110

Reject useless conventions
Showed me my father's grave
And buried my mother with grace
Roses are red
Violet is my mother.

SAILING AWAY

I am failing to resonate with reality
Like this world is not my home
I feel lonely
There must be a place somewhere
Faraway
Where the sun doesn't glare at my failures
Shining cold in summer
Hot in winter
Where the moon doesn't leer at my
Loneliness
The wind doesn't blow the air away
A place I can stay and live every day.
I am sailing away
Sailing away

They came in my dreams
Except they were not dreams but nightmares
Beautiful fourth dimension scenery
A place time stood still for a thrill
A place where the pain is pleasure
Gold is a base treasure
And I get to exist and not just to live
A place I get and get and never give
Can't wait for the ship
Can't wait to fly away
The flying saucer
I am sailing away
Sailing away.

SAY IT

Be careful what you are told as the truth
Human beings are morbid peddlers of untruth
Always slanting the truth for own purpose
Truth hangs in limbo in the smoke of lies on purpose
I have met preacher man twisting the truth to suit a
narrative
So it is important to know that truth is relative
Scriptures and history books are perfect records of
wishful unreality
Convoluted reality

Even in this day of tech advancement
People brazenly lie for advantage
Weapons of mass destruction
The truth in reconstruction
See where these lies led us
And not a single person makes a fuss
Everyone carrying on as if the manufactured consent is
right
Truth bombed out of sight

For a bard
It is hard
Not to venture an opinion
Putting history on a rack and pinion
Causing some discomfort
The truth comes forth
You may become the proverbial renegade
Smile and drink your energies

Don't let the truth die
No lie

Let those who cry cry
Those who try try
To bend the truth for profit
Bard has none of it
You might be treated as a pariah in future
A misfit living in discomfiture

So be it
Say it

SAY WHAT?

Spring sprung
Winter wilted
Autumn automated
Summer sighed

Dis year dismissed
Last year lasted
Next year nixed
All years old

Every month manic
Every week weak
Every day gay
Every year yeah!

An hour ours
A minute mean it
A second record
A day say, say what?

A SCHISM

Cryptically thinking
A tree growing the leaves underground
The roots above ground.
Reverse photosynthesis
The thesis this is efil...maybe this is life
Topsy turvy
Thoughts detracted, curvy
Air pollution containing food
Good radioactive gooey
Gamma rays ionizing powerful
The roots green and colourful
The leaves rusty brown
Rotting in the ground
The tree trunk drunk with cancerferrous toxicity from
the shitty city.

Orifices sealed filled killed cells merged
Humaniodity submerged converged on the verge
Appendages in air digital digits floating oil slick slime
lime in time
The sole soul food.
Single-celled
Life thrives
Fate in a vacuum
An impossibility
An improbability

Critically thinking
There's life after death
The antimatter
The antilife
Discreation discretion of creation

116

Preponderant life
In the multiverse
Single-celled nanosized behemoth
Wallowing in a selfish self-fulfilling wishful wish wash
We exist
We don't
We exit
We won't
We can't
Closed system
Schism

117

SCIENCE

Let's talk about science
It does not help to be silent
A lot of people think science is experimentation
Granted in science there is fermentation
But, there is a broader definition
One that does not involve premonition
Science is the sum total of all things that support life
This is the definition that works, but superstition is rife

Have we humans exhausted the study of science?
We haven't even started to unravel its mysteries, its
salience
Have we made our short stay here on earth
comfortable?
Genetically modified meat into vegetables?
Have we found ways to improve our longevity?
Researched to increase our vitality?

The answer to all these questions is no
We don't know what we should and must know.
Yet we claim to know things that don't add value to our
lives
Things that cause us to fight with our knives
We spend millions on spiritual stuff as if we are spirits
Why do spiritual stuff when you are human like you can
feel it?
Before you were born did you have consciousness
Why do you want consciousness when you are dead;
unconscious
Is it not better to deal with spiritual stuff when you
become so?
And rather spend time doing science till you know

It is a fallacious excuse to say God wants this or that
God created science and the lack of use of science is
contra
We have been given a short life to live on this earth
Rather than making use of the time to live life before
death,
We spend time killing, enslaving, oppressing, raping in
the name of religion
We pretend to know God like we are doves when we
are pigeons
I daresay if you look at all the wars and conflicts since
history was recorded they are based on a faith
One people want to subjugate another because "god"
told them so in their face.

If we utilize the science that God created for us that is
sufficient thanksgiving, not all these prayers
Reciting books, playing politics, and abusing God's name
to achieve superiority and dominion over others,
nothing to do with God! It's the game of players.
Science and religion

Science will silence dreams in sub-conscience
Tyrants will cause screams subcontinents
They show you the way
The endless highway
Engineers, builder subcontractor

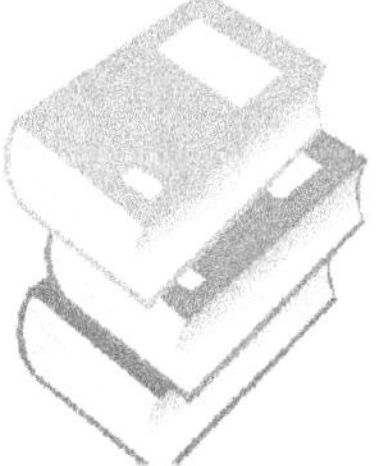

SCIENCE AND RELIGION

Show me where faith has worked
Completed any project on time
I will show you where it caused havoc
Every line doesn't have to rhyme
Newton's laws are not based on faith
Charles Darwin theories are not fact
Einstein had faith but used science
And his theory caused belief silence
Nothing works without laws of nature
Despite gaining political stature
The reality is we still need air to breathe
Even procreation we do need to breed
Laws of nature are the Laws of God
In these laws, we find the atom of Gold
God is too Omni important to be elated
In our prayers and the hymns created
Our creator rejoices in the love shown
Not in the hatred and killing of his own

SCOOBY DO

Here, there, everywhere, no one is aware
Heavy heart, lump in the throat, no one is there
You are all alone
No one to atone
Don't panic, call Scooby Do, he cares

HEAVY HEART

H-eave a sigh of relief
E-ven now is the time for belief
A-nd accept that though you re alone
V-ery close is someone to tell to atone
Y-ou don't see him
H-is power is in the hymn
E-veryone has heard his name
A-cross the globe it's the same
R-evel in the power of Jesus of God
T-he Man, you need when you feel cold

LUMP IN YOUR THROAT

Get a life and cheer up
Be the big dog not the pup
When the world short changes you
Friends treat you like a fool
Non-friends rub salt into your sore
Don't waste time taking a snore
Dress up in your favourite coat
Go drink away the lump in your throat

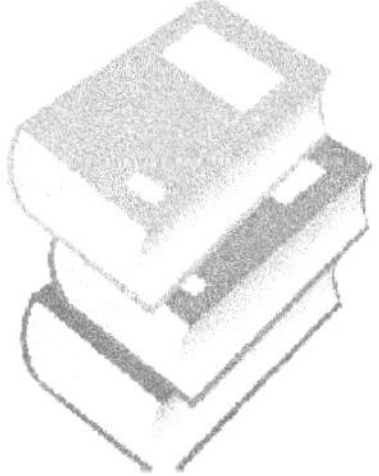

SEQUENCES

They said there would be consequences
All he saw were events in sequences
She was beautiful
His love bountiful
Chain reaction gave morning sicknesses

CONSEQUENCES

Conrad the con artist arranged his corn in sequences
There was white corn, yellow corn, and green corn
wrapped in porn sin scenes
The morality police came to greet Conrad
He drove away in his Ford along the corn road

Consequences

Consider the effect before you do
Only then should you make a move
Never underestimate a reaction
Some have taken rushed action
Ended up in a quagmire
Quite messy nothing to admire
Until you have done a full analysis
Everything including possible catalyst
Not all quiescent situations are quiet
Consider chain reactions salient
Each scenario catered for
Serious sequences are known before

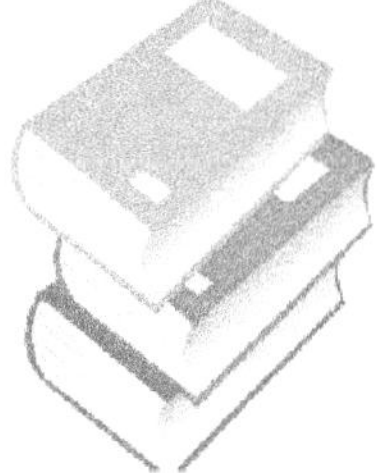

SERENDIPITY

Trinity is truly infinity
Some have spent years studying divinity
Curiosity kills
Religiosity thrills
Serendipity is serenity

Serendipity

S-ee how nature gives
E-nabling us to live
R-elatively well
E-ven quite a swell
N-ot knowing where cometh blessings
D-espite events that is depressing
I-n our lives living with stress
P-eriods of unexpected distress
I-t is incumbent upon us
T-o be thankful and trust
Y-ears of bliss and serendipity

- - - - - - - - - - - - - - - - -

What about infinity it's full of fools with divinity.

- - - - - - - - - - - - - - - - -

THE SILENCE IN THE NOISE

What would you rather have?
Pretentious just to behave?
Or to have the truth out in the open?
Some people lie all too often
Causing unnecessary energy
Causing even an allergy
The truth never changes
Doesn't matter who gets the rages
But, once the truth is known
People make decisions of their own

The sun rises in the east, sets in the west
That is true no matter your quest
We need air to breathe
But, we can live without a breeze
These are facts and we live with them
Even other things in life are the same
It is not what you believe to be true is the truth
Between your beliefs and truth is the truce
The point at which forces of nature support you
If forces of nature do not support you start anew

Manufactured consent is just that
If you take it as truth you fall flat
Find the real truth even in a rose
It might be the silence in the noise

127

THE SILENCE OF SCIENCE

Forgive me father I have seen
Everywhere I have been
They kneel to pray to you
And claim they know you
Talk to you
And that they are coming to you
Yet the air we breathe is you
The earth we still is you
Every creature is you
You gave us science
The silence of science
To derive all we need
Out of greed, beyond our need
We destroy them in your name
Without shame.
Forgive me, father I have been
Everywhere I have seen.
The lack of science
The lack of silence
People turning to philosophy
Religions full of apostrophe
Apostles
Father, I am amazed
Even fazed
Mortals feign annoyance
With arrogance
On your behalf
In a huff

Despite the threat of judgment day.
When they say, you will have your say.
See the big churches they build
With diamonds, they form a guild
See the millions of souls they pull
The hapless flock they fool
What has that to do with you?
I wish I knew.
Yet you are quiet
Silent
The silence of science.

BE SILENT

Human beings are a semi-intelligent species
You can pick the self-loathing and doublespeak in
speeches
So to calm their phobia of expiring back to nature
They create in their minds heaven and hell and the
rapture
This whole obsession with deity and religion
Demonstrates a recession from reality like a pigeon
Sent to deliver a message of "Save our souls"
Pretends it knows the soul of a guinea fowl

Yet life works because of science
We breathe because of science
We exist because we are supported by science
All the laws of nature are all science
The beginning of life is science
The solar system works in science
We are able to replicate a human with science
Help me say it loud and clear don't, be silent.

Let's do science
Life is science
Death is science
The universe is science
Black holes are science
Pandemics is science
Even God is science
Religion be silent

SILENT KILLER

It's not Aids
It's not expired meds
It's not diabetes
Or any other myelitis
It's not hypertension
Or shortages of angiotensin's
Not even malaria
Anophillus in the area
It's not poverty
Caused by stolen property
Not even car accidents
Horrific road incidents
Plane crashes
Or war clashes
Don't blame wild animals
The big five mammals

Here is the thriller
The silent killer
Is ignorance
A preponderance of ignoramuses
With education
The panacea, our problem eradication
Educate your kids
This is what they need
In the future to live in peace
All over, even in Athens, Greece
If people were properly schooled
No one would, with propaganda, be fooled.
These are my pleas
Do it please!

131

THRILLER

"Incubus" a thriller watched as a filler
A killer silently tried to kill her
Came with a big knife
Tried to end her life
She screamed at her hubby, "Silent Killer! "

Silent killer

Rufus was a big burly shabby rough guy
Women turned back or changed path he wondered why
One day a sexy lady dressed in red met Rufus looking
rough
"Hello," she said seductively "My name be Succubus! "

Silent killer

"Silent killer! "
Such a thriller
Coming to a big screen.
In your bedroom, don't scream
It's just a dream
It's not real

SILENT NIGHT

133

There is a specific day. A specific night. Moon full. A moon playing hide and seek with owls, rodents, and other nightly creatures. A night with cotton wool-like wispy clouds passing in front of an irritated moon. The air completely still as if the earth is holding its breath in anticipation of something. Something which happens on this specific day. On this specific night. On this particular night of the full moon and deathly silence, it's the same dream. The dream of a shadowy figure silhouetted against the moon. Whenever the clouds pass in front of the bemused moon there is a blood-curdling howl. Without fail the dream recurs on a specific day. On a specific night. Silent night howling night.

SINS, WARTS AND ALL

If you are black, white, or yellow
You are a woman or a fellow
Or any of the states of humanity
Lame, maimed, or in a secret community
Doesn't matter you are at the mall
God loves you, sins, warts and all

If you have committed a serious crime
Behaved like God killing people every time
Or any of the sins stated in the Book
Coveted, lied, adultery you undertook
Doesn't matter repent get up from your fall
God loves you, sins, warts and all

Come ye to God, sins, warts and all
Come all nations, sins, warts and all

SISTERS

Lizzie Borden

Sisters sizzle with zeal to assist us
Your sibling your kids can usually fuss
Very reliable
Was she liable?
Lizzie Borden took ax gave blows so don't trust?

Lizzie Borden

Lizzie gave sisters a bad name
Including innocents all the same
Zeal is shown when telling a story
Zealots adding stuff to make it gory
In reality, she went scot-free
Everyone disagreed even you and me
But our own sisters are good
Our kids love them though rude
We let our sisters help with our kids
Defending brothers when morals skid
Eve may have lost to one Lucifer
Not all our beautiful sisters thus far

SLEEPING PILL

The thrill in the shrill will trill on the scene
Still, there is no will to give up the fill
She be screaming
You be dreaming
Dreaming binge her shouting a sleeping pill

Sleeping pill

Sleep deprivation is bad news
Leaving your mind with sad views
Every evening a disappointment
Every day a bad development
Pills help but can be addictive
In the morning you are reactive
Not coherent not composed
Going to drink is totally opposed
People end up alcoholics
In the same league as chocoholics
Look to your spouse in the house
Look to them the ache they douse

Sleeping pill

My shouts out to all people with chronicle illness
Those that depend on drugs for their fitness
Perhaps you have chronic cancer
Medicine has failed to find a permanent answer
Perhaps something like chronic alcohol abuse

136

You have tried the AA or herbs, but it's no use
Perhaps you suffer a nervous system milady
Chronic pain when you drive the Honda Ballade
To you all my fellow humans, yours is a heroic existence
Considering the demands on life's little insistences
Sleeping pills often allow you to rest easy
Other drugs like cocaine making you queasy
Alcohol helps, but long term causing dependence
When ultimately you want freedom and independence
I just wanna say whatever be your affliction
At PH we feel for you and have love and affection
Never ever give up, go on and on
You are not gone until you are gone

"SO WHAT? "

I work all day to bring food to the table,
Make my wife and kids comfortable
I work the night shift,
Even work on a night ship.
But, when I think it's all going to end,
When I say goodbye to my friend
I ask myself what all this is in aid of
All this pain when I work my butt off
I come to the "So what? " Moment
The "So what? " question. My torment

I even try to be nice
Offer a drink with ice
And be-friend all the people I meet
Everywhere I go on the street
The feeling I get is the same
The feeling of playing the same game It's the same "So what? " moment
The "So what? " question. My torment.

SOMEONE'S CHILD

I have seen emaciated ghostly-looking children. I think
they are, children. I think they are someone's child
forsaken.

They live on the edge of the river
The raw water reeking of sewage,
Carrying flotsam of deadly disease. Here, the ghostly
figures gleefully woefully recreate. Like I said, I think
they are children. I think they are someone's child
forsaken.

A lost generation condemned to perpetual hunger,
Hunger whose causal rationale they do not understand.
Born in the streets, sleeping in the sewers.
When they succumb to preventable disease, their
comrades-in-suffering simply shove them in the river,
And go back to their cherished sewer abodes where
they sleep,
Piled up like bales of tobacco,
Oft times never to wake up.

Like I said, I think they are children. Someone's child
forsaken.

The state doesn't know them. They never got a birth
certificate. When they die there is no death certificate.
Therefore, there is no problem.

But, like I said, I think they are children. Someone's child
forsaken.

Orphans abused often,

139

Ignored by their parents,
Ignored by miracle-working pastors
Ignored by pot-bellied politicians
Ignored by the state
Ignored by Africa,
Ignored by the world.

Someone's child forsaken. I think they are children.

SOMEONE I NEVER KNEW

I write more than I talk
It's like taking a walk
A literary prowess lying dormant
Like Mount Etna erupts
Then suddenly sleeps again
Like Auntie Etina was abrupt
Appeared as sudden as rain
Then disappeared forever
Someone I never knew

Words paint a picture so clear
Causing eyes to drop a tear
Like plumes of sulfur dioxide
Like Krakatoa exploding
Running away in fear
Your heart imploding
Afraid of words so clear
Like Auntie Budisai ran away
Someone I never knew

Words flowing over valleys
Over rivers and gulleys
Pouring forth like a fountain
After years of quiet
Like Mt Kilimanjaro is silent
Suddenly to jolt your ears
You strap your suckling twins
And run away in tears
Like Auntie Chifedza did
Someone I never knew

141

SOME.......

Somehow there is life within death
That's how things rebirth themselves

Somewhere on this earth, there is death happening
A living thing succumbing to the excesses of nature

Someone is losing consciousness for the last time
Leaving behind whatever it was they held dear.

Something is replacing that which has expired even as I
write this.
The sea becoming land, land flooding with water

Somewhat, there are things we take for granted
because our lives are short
Even the sun, the earth, and the moon will renew their
ending.

Someday, somehow, everything will come to an end
due to something from somewhere.

SOCIETY EXPECTS

Lonely I feel only when you are here with me.

When you are gone, gone is my one and only moment of feigning affection.

I feel nothing in my void of nothingness, having loved myself first alone.

Ostensibly, you came to occupy my sane senses with intangible feelings of affection. A fiat only existing through repetition and repertoire. You say 'I love you' so many times that I now believe I love you too. But, I feel satiety in solitude. My alone moments the best lonely moments sans comments.

Rather, I savour vivid videos in my mind of erotic fantasies I gratuitously steal from moments of voyeur in abstentia. Pure bliss laced with lucid hallucinations of memories of murmurings and musings in music. Super psychedelic psychotropic entanglements. The stochastic feelings are to me an evolution revolution.

So, now, therefore, I say to you,

Every time you tell me you love me, I say I love you too because society expects me to say that. So, ok, ok, I love you too.

143

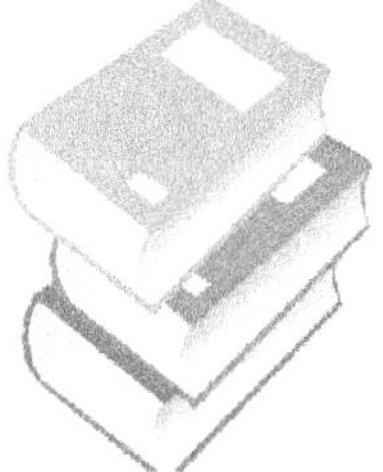

SOMETIMES IN ANGER, THERE IS TRUTH.

Sometimes in anger, there is truth
A person you thought was a friend
When you are not there behaves uncouth

He smiles when you are there, behind says you are a
fool
Displays so much anger
Sometimes in anger, there is truth

He is quick, about you, to speak untruth
Pretends he knows a lot more about you
When you are not there behaves uncouth

His patronizing jokes are crude
To bring your reputation to his level
Sometimes in anger, there is truth

When you are in a bad mood
He sheds fake crocodile tears
When you are not there behaves uncouth

His morbid jealousy of you is understood
He works hard to display his anger
When you are not there behaves uncouth
Sometimes in anger, there is truth.

144

SOUL SEARCHING

I am looking for my soul
On my anatomy, I can't find it
Not in my brain
Nor in my heart
Not even in my gut

Perhaps if I could turn my eyes
In their sockets and look inside
If I could I would
But I doubt I would find it.
They keep telling me to look inside my soul

Is it a collection of memories etched on my mind?
Is it resident in the synapsis in my brain?

They say some people have no soul
No mercy
No compunction
They take life
With a knife
Or a gun
For them it's fun.

I don't do such
Not that much
But I still can't find my soul
Not at all

145

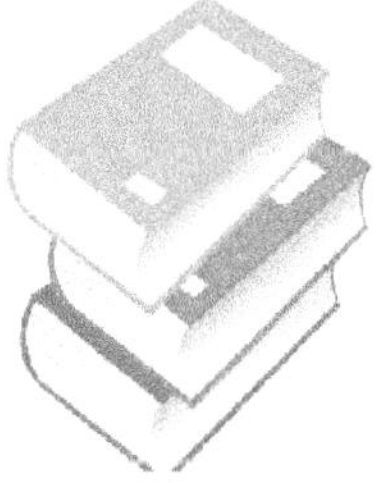

ABOUT THE AUTHOR

DELUKE MUWANIGWA

"I am a novice Zimbabwean poet learning the ropes. Though my profession is engineering I find myself drawn to literature, particularly poetry. This book contains my poems written over some time in my lonely moments as I watched the world turning and turning and people praying and praying. I hope you will enjoy it."